Original title:

Glassy Fissures Under the Dragon Spray

Author: Kätriin Kaldaru

ISBN HARDBACK: 978-1-80559-288-4

ISBN PAPERBACK: 978-1-80559-787-2

Fragments of Serenity in Turmoil

In chaos' grip, a hush remains,
Where whispers dance with fleeting gain.
Each heartbeat calm, amidst the strife,
A gentle beam, the pulse of life.

The storm may rage, the winds may howl,
Yet there, a stillness does avowel.
In fractured moments, peace is found,
A sacred space, profound, unbound.

Blue skies peep through the tempest's veil,
Soft reminders that love prevails.
Every tear a crystal clear,
Echoes of joy that reappear.

In nature's hand, a fragile grace,
Serenity's glow, a warm embrace.
Through turmoil's lens, the heart will see,
The beauty crafted, wild and free.

Amongst the ruins, life will bloom,
A wildflower sweetening the gloom.
In scattered shards of silent light,
Fragments of hope gleam through the night.

Luminous Breaths in the Roaring Dive

As shadows fade beneath the tide,
The waters sing, their secrets wide.
In depths where silence holds its reign,
Luminous breaths break through the pain.

The ocean's pulse, a rhythmic sway,
Guiding lost souls along the way.
In currents swift, they find their course,
Embraced by waves, a mighty force.

Colors shimmer, glimmers bright,
Turning darkness into light.
Each drop a gem, a dance divine,
In currents where the stars align.

The roaring dive, a wild embrace,
Yet in the chaos, beauty's trace.
Breaths of courage, soft and true,
Illuminate the ocean's blue.

Waves whisper tales of ancient lore,
Lessons learned from those before.
In luminous depths, find solace deep,
In the roaring dive, our spirits leap.

Phantom Secrets Beneath the Surface

In shadowed realms where whispers dwell,
Phantom secrets weave their spell.
Beneath the calm, a storm may brew,
Truths obscured, yet calling you.

Ripples form in sacred streams,
Echoing our buried dreams.
Through tangled roots, the past will creep,
Secrets hidden, memories steep.

In twilight's glow, the veil is thin,
Where light and dark begin to spin.
Flickers of fate dance in the night,
Enigmas glow with tender light.

Each heartbeat pulses with the lore,
Of phantom truths that seek the shore.
In silent depths, the heart does ache,
For revelations yet to break.

So delve into the depths unseen,
Uncover tales that weave between.
For in the dark, the light does shine,
Phantom secrets, yours and mine.

Glistening Shadows in the Torrent

In torrents fierce, the waters churn,
Glistening shadows twist and turn.
Silent whispers ride the foam,
In nature's fury, we find home.

Each drop a tale, a story spun,
Of battles lost and victories won.
In swirling tides, reflections glide,
Glistening shadows, a wild ride.

The river flows with ancient grace,
Mirroring the ever-changing face.
Beneath the roar, soft echoes hide,
In these shadows, secrets bide.

Through tempest's rage, the heart will beat,
Finding solace in the heat.
As shadows dance in water's light,
The torrent reveals its inner sight.

In every wave, a chance to rise,
Glistening shadows paint our skies.
So let us plunge into the storm,
For in the chaos, we transform.

Celestial Whispers Beneath the Cascades

Stars dance lightly in the night,
Gentle winds cradle dreams in flight.
Whispers echo through the trees,
Nature's song floats on the breeze.

Moonlit paths reveal the way,
As shadows blend with night and day.
Waterfalls sing a timeless tune,
In harmony with silver moon.

Crystals shimmer on the ground,
In this magic, peace is found.
Each drop sparkles, a shooting star,
Guiding lost souls from afar.

The air is thick with sweet perfume,
Life unfolds in every bloom.
Celestial light, a soft embrace,
Wraps the world in its grace.

Every moment, pure delight,
Beneath the stars, a fleeting night.
Cascades whisper, soft and low,
Carrying dreams where rivers flow.

Awakening Shadows in the Mist

Fog rolls in, a ghostly shroud,
Veiling whispers, soft and loud.
Shadows stretch and intertwine,
Mornings break with tales divine.

Dew-kissed petals greet the dawn,
In silence, every thought's reborn.
Nature holds a breath of grace,
As the sun begins its chase.

Each step reveals a hidden path,
Where secrets lie, and echoes laugh.
The mist embraces all it finds,
In tender dance, where fate unwinds.

Light weaves through the smoky gray,
Illuminating the soft ballet.
Creatures stir in hushed repose,
As the world begins to rose.

Awakening life, a brand-new start,
Melding dreams with the beating heart.
In shadows' breath, a soft reprise,
Life unfurls beneath clear skies.

Fragments of Forgotten Souls

Whispers linger in the air,
Echoes of a silent prayer.
Forgotten dreams on dusty shelves,
Tales of what we once called selves.

In corners dark, the past unspools,
Woven tales of ancient fools.
Silent cries of love and pain,
Fragments lost in memory's stain.

Each moment holds a story dear,
Captured glimmers, crystal clear.
In shadows cast by flickering light,
We seek the truth in endless night.

Ghosts of laughter, tears of sorrow,
Sculpting futures, shaping tomorrow.
In every sigh, a life unfolds,
In fragments, whispers of old souls.

As time flows like a river's grace,
We find our home in every space.
Piecing together what once was whole,
In sacred dance, we heal the soul.

Essence of Dusk on Liquid Glass

The sun dips low, a golden hue,
Painting skies in shades anew.
Rippling waters catch the glow,
Reflecting dreams that gently flow.

Crimson edges kiss the night,
As stars awaken, sharing light.
Whispers soft upon the lake,
Breeze carries tales that night will make.

Each wave dances, a fleeting trace,
Drawing hearts into the grace.
Dusk reveals a tranquil peace,
In liquid glass, all troubles cease.

Nature holds its breath in awe,
As day departs, a sacred law.
Essence lingers, sweet and bold,
In twilight's arms, stories told.

Time slows down in evening's gaze,
Lost in the beauty of the phase.
Liquid glass reflects the past,
In every moment, shadows cast.

Dragon's Breath on a Silver Canvas

Across the dusk, the shadows glide,
A dragon's breath, a fierce and wild ride.
In silver hues, the stars ignite,
Unraveling dreams in the cloak of night.

Wings of wonder, soaring high,
Painting stories across the sky.
In twilight's whisper, secrets spin,
A dance of sparks where joy begins.

With every roar, the silence breaks,
In every heart, a fire awakes.
The canvas glows with vibrant light,
Holding tales of love and fright.

As night unfolds its mystic charms,
The dragon's breath in open arms.
A fleeting moment, captured still,
In silver strokes, our dreams fulfill.

Reflections of a Storm-Kissed Heart

Beneath the rain, emotions swell,
A storm-kissed heart, with tales to tell.
Mirrored droplets fall and gleam,
Fragments of a forgotten dream.

Thunder rumbles, a lover's sigh,
In gentle whispers, the winds comply.
Lightning dances, electric grace,
Illuminating every trace.

Through tempest's rage, we find our peace,
In chaos, longing only increases.
Reflections cast on waters wide,
Emotions swell, like the rising tide.

With every gust, a longing grows,
The storm reveals what stillness knows.
A heart set free, yet bound by fate,
In storm's embrace, we celebrate.

Secrets Laid Bare Beneath the Sea

In ocean depths, the secrets hide,
Whispers of ancient worlds confined.
Coral castles, silent and grand,
Hold stories lost in shifting sand.

Bubbles rise like dreams set free,
Carried by currents, wild and free.
In shadows dance the mermaid's song,
Echoing where our hearts belong.

Treasure chests in darkened beds,
Wonders where the siren treads.
Beneath the waves, a tapestry,
Of wild and wistful mystery.

Secrets laid bare, and yet unseen,
In depths where light meets evergreen.
With every wave, a story flows,
In drifts and tides, the ocean knows.

The Dance of Light Amidst the Tempest

In swirling winds, the lanterns sway,
A dance of light amidst the gray.
Flickers bright against the storm,
Guiding souls in search of warm.

Each ray a promise, bold and true,
In shadows cast, the hope breaks through.
With every gust, a sparkle gleams,
A waltz of fate, igniting dreams.

Through raging tides, our spirits leap,
A rhythm found where silence sleeps.
In chaos lies a cosmic hand,
Leading us to a brighter land.

The tempest roars, yet we will stand,
With hearts entwined, we'll make our plan.
For in the storm, we find our grace,
A dance of light in time and space.

Violet Ripples on an Ancient Lake

Violet ripples dance like dreams,
Upon the lake where silence gleams.
Soft whispers float upon the air,
Carried by winds, both light and rare.

Each splash tells tales long left unsaid,
Of timeless journeys, hopes that led.
Reflections shimmer with a glow,
In twilight's arms, where shadows flow.

The moon dips low, a silver thread,
Weaving wishes to the waterbed.
Crickets chirp their night-time song,
In harmony where hearts belong.

Stars emerge like scattered dreams,
Painting stories in luminous beams.
The lake, a mirror to the night,
Holds every secret out of sight.

As silence falls, the world feels still,
Nature's breath a gentle thrill.
In violet hues, peace doth arise,
Beneath the canvas of the skies.

Crystalline Echoes in the Gloom

In twilight's shroud, soft echoes ring,
Crystalline whispers start to sing.
Fragments of light through branches peep,
In shadows deep, where secrets sleep.

The world grows quiet, the air is thick,
With stories woven, a subtle trick.
Each note a glimmer, each sigh a tear,
In the gloom, their voices near.

Moonbeams twirl in a waltz of grace,
Illuminating this hidden space.
Glistening thoughts in the darkened haze,
Guide lost souls through their winding maze.

Muffled footfalls on the forest floor,
Echoes linger, forevermore.
In this embrace of soft dismay,
Crystalline dreams shimmer and sway.

As night unfolds its velvet shawl,
Ancient shadows rise and fall.
Each moment captured, frozen in time,
Whispers of beauty, a silent chime.

Veins of Light Amidst the Shadows

Veins of light twist through the dark,
Breaching shadows with a spark.
Like fireflies in sultry air,
They dance and shimmer, bright and rare.

Every corner holds a sigh,
Breath of dusk, a muted cry.
Flickering hope breaks through the night,
Illuminating endless flight.

Ghostly figures form and fade,
In alleyways where dreams are laid.
Each flicker tells a tale of old,
Of hearts brave and spirits bold.

With whispered love in shadows cast,
Moments merge, both slow and fast.
Light weaves stories, tender and true,
Bringing warmth where chilling flew.

Veins of light in twilight merge,
Creating paths where dreams emerge.
Awakening wonders that softly play,
In the canvas of night, they sway.

Whispers of Secrets in the Cascade

In the cascade, secrets flow,
Whispers ride the currents low.
Water speaks in gentle tones,
Sharing tales of ancient stones.

Leaves dance lightly in the breeze,
Carrying echoes through the trees.
Each drop a memory, soft and clear,
Murmuring stories for those who hear.

Sunlight glints on the surface bright,
Revealing shadows kissed by light.
The melody of rippling sound,
In every corner, truth is found.

Beneath the rush, a world does thrive,
Where life awakens, feels alive.
The whispering waters, a sweet refrain,
Flowing freely, devoid of pain.

With every turn, the secrets flow,
In the cascade, hearts start to grow.
Nature's language, pure and vast,
Forever speaking, forever cast.

Misty Secrets of the Serpent's Trail

In the hush of morning's light,
Whispers dance upon the breeze.
Winding paths through trees so tight,
Tell of secrets, heart's unease.

Shadows play on dampened ground,
Softly curling, veiling fate.
Eyes of wonder, lost, unbound,
Seeking truths that hearts await.

Misty trails of emerald hue,
Lead to places deeply scarred.
In the fog, a vision true,
Lies the wisdom found and hard.

Echoes of the past remain,
In each step, a story weaves.
Through the quiet, through the pain,
Nature's lore, the heart perceives.

To the serpent's song we bend,
Following with careful grace.
In the end, we find a friend,
In the mist and hidden space.

The Enchantment of Icy Waters

Flows a stream with crystal glow,
Mirrored skies, a tranquil scene.
Underneath, the wonders flow,
Secrets glide where none have been.

Frigid depths that hold their lore,
In the silence, fables sleep.
Every ripple, evermore,
Keeps within its grasp so deep.

Frozen edges sparkle bright,
Kissed by frost in morning's breath.
Casting glimmers into night,
Whispers soft of life and death.

Gentle currents, soft embrace,
Draw us near with silent call.
In the water, find our place,
Feel the magic, hear it all.

Icy mountains watch and wait,
Guardians of this hidden world.
In their shadows, we create,
Threads of tales yet to be twirled.

Veils of Vapor and Twilight Fire

In the dusk, the colors blend,
Veils of mist, a soft caress.
As the daylight meets its end,
Twilight flames begin to press.

Shadows stretch and softly dance,
Flickers bright in violet skies.
In the dreamlike, take a chance,
Feel the magic as it flies.

Whispers linger on the air,
Filled with stories from the night.
Every breath a tender prayer,
As the stars ignite their light.

Vapor trails in winding form,
Guide the heart toward the fire.
In this moment, feel the warm,
Hearts igniting with desire.

Here in twilight's gentle hold,
Find the peace that seeks to bloom.
In this cradle, tales unfold,
Veils of dreams within the gloom.

Celestial Echoes in the Glassy Deep

Beneath the waves, a silence sings,
Celestial dreams in gleaming blue.
Every ripple softly brings,
Tales of stars and skies anew.

In the depths, where shadows play,
Echoes call from far away.
Time stands still, a fluid sway,
Cradled in the ocean's gray.

Glistening realms, a world apart,
Songs of worlds beneath the swell.
Every heartbeat is a part,
Of a wondrous, ancient spell.

As we dive, the mystics show,
Secrets of the deep unfold.
In the depths, we come to know,
Stories whispered, brave and bold.

Celestial echoes, catching light,
In the glassy, endless sea.
Here, we find our souls take flight,
With each wave, we are set free.

Reflections of Eternity in Motion

Time dances lightly, feet on air,
Moments captured, fading, rare.
Whispers of ages, soft and bright,
Echoing softly, day into night.

Stars twinkle gently in cosmic streams,
Woven together are time's lost dreams.
Each heartbeat pulses, a story told,
In the tapestry of the young and old.

Fleeting shadows weave through the trees,
Carried on whispers, carried on breeze.
The past in motion, the future near,
In this dance of life, we persevere.

Moments collide, catch my breath,
In the beauty of life, we conquer death.
Eternity spins through this fragile time,
All is connected, all in rhyme.

Flow of the Heart in Nature's Grasp

Gentle streams murmur, softly they flow,
Nature's embrace where wildflowers grow.
Hearts beat to rhythms of rustling leaves,
Whispering secrets that the forest weaves.

Sunlight dapples through the emerald trees,
Painting the path where the spirit finds ease.
Each petal and breeze shares a story anew,
Inviting the heart's love to blossom and bloom.

Mountains rise high with their heads in the sky,
Cradling echoes of dreams that fly by.
Rivers of gold spill beneath the tall pine,
Guiding the heart where the wild spirits shine.

In stillness, the soul hears the call of the land,
Finding its rhythm, a heartbeat so grand.
Together we move, in harmony's dance,
Nature surrounds, granting us a chance.

Twilight's Embrace on the Water's Edge

As twilight descends, the water glows,
A canvas painted with the day's last throws.
Reflections shimmer, dreams intertwine,
Under the gaze of the evening's design.

Waves softly whisper, kissing the shore,
Secrets of twilight, yearning for more.
Stars awaken, one by one,
Embracing the night, with day now done.

The pulse of the water, a rhythmic sigh,
Holding my heart as the night's spirit flies.
Melodies linger, the world drifts away,
In twilight's embrace, I long to stay.

Moonlight dances on ripples of fate,
Guiding our dreams through the waters so late.
With each heartbeat, our spirits align,
In the twilight's magic, forever entwined.

Siren's Song in the Misty Currents

In the misty currents, a call from the deep,
Echoes of beauty that stir while we sleep.
Siren's sweet song, haunting and clear,
Wooing the wanderers, drawing them near.

Whispers of water float on the breeze,
Carrying secrets through ancient trees.
Lost in the melody, hearts start to sway,
Pulled by the longing of the ocean's display.

Misty horizons fade into night,
A shimmering beacon, lost in the light.
In silence they beckon with tales of the bold,
Woven in rhythms of wonders untold.

Tides churn and shift, with every refrain,
Guiding the way through joy and through pain.
Sing to the moon, let the currents unfold,
In the siren's embrace, our spirits behold.

Invisible Threads in the Heart of Storms

In shadows deep, the whispers rise,
Invisible threads weave through the skies.
Caught in the dance of thunder's might,
Hearts beat softly, embracing the night.

Fingers trace paths where echoes hum,
In every drop, a world becomes.
Lightning flickers, a fleeting spark,
In storm's embrace, we find our mark.

Raindrops fall like ancient tears,
Each one holding all our fears.
Yet through the haze of tempest's wails,
Love's tethered light never fails.

Amidst the chaos, a calm will bloom,
In wounded hearts, the wild consumes.
Beneath the roar, we gather strength,
Invisible threads, an endless length.

In the eye of the storm, peace can be found,
A quiet pulse in the battleground.
Together we tread, through sorrow and bliss,
For in every storm, there's a whispered kiss.

Radiant Secrets of the Whispering Clyde

By the river's edge, the willows sigh,
Secrets dance in the breeze that sighs.
Whispers flow where the waters gleam,
As twilight brings forth a gentle dream.

Stars reflect on the rippling stream,
Scattered like thoughts in a starlit beam.
Each wave carries a tale untold,
Of lovers lost and visions bold.

In the hush of night, shadows softly creep,
Guarding the treasures that the river keeps.
Moonlight bathes the path in grace,
Where memories linger, time won't erase.

The Clyde softly hums a familiar tune,
Crickets join in beneath the moon.
Nature's symphony, a soothing balm,
Wrapped in the night, it feels so calm.

Beneath the surface, the mystery swirls,
Tales woven deep in the heart of pearls.
The river flows on, its secrets tight,
Radiant truths hold the world in light.

Twilight Hues on Nature's Canvas

As day gives way to night's embrace,
Twilight paints in a tender grace.
Brush strokes of orange, purple, and gold,
Nature's canvas, stories unfold.

The whispering breeze carries soft sighs,
Birds take flight as the daylight dies.
Dusk settles in with a gentle hand,
Cradling the world, a spell so grand.

Stars awaken in the velvet sky,
Each one a gem that dares to fly.
In this quiet, magic blooms unseen,
A dance of shadows, a world serene.

Mountains bathed in the evening glow,
The rivers shimmer as soft winds blow.
In these twilight hues, our hearts align,
Drawing us close to what is divine.

Moments linger where dreams reside,
In nature's hush, we cast aside,
The noise of life, finding peace anew,
In twilight hues, life feels true.

Life Beneath the Roar of Winds

Among the trees, the wind does speak,
Rustling leaves as they bend and creak.
Each gust carries whispers from afar,
Secrets held close, beneath each star.

Roots sink deep in the earthen soil,
Life pushes forth, enduring toil.
Through tempests fierce, they sway and bend,
In every struggle, we find a friend.

Branches reach high, longing for light,
Dancing boldly in the heart of night.
Amidst the chaos, they find their way,
Life reborn with each new day.

In the loudest storms, we learn to trust,
To weather the fierce, rise from the dust.
For beneath the roar, there is a song,
A melody soft, where we all belong.

With every breeze, a tale unfolds,
A story of strength, a journey bold.
Life beneath the winds, a daring call,
In nature's arms, we will not fall.

The Dance of Water and Light

Ripples glisten in the sun,
A shimmering ballet begun.
Water twirls in joyful grace,
Reflecting light's warm embrace.

Dancing droplets take their flight,
Echoes of a world so bright.
Their whispers play on gentle winds,
As day and night become good friends.

Colors shift and softly blend,
In each curve, a message penned.
Nature's canvas comes alive,
In water's dance, the spirits thrive.

The stream pirouettes along,
In nature's rhythm, a sweet song.
Where light meets water's soft caress,
The heart finds peace, the soul's recess.

Together they weave a tale,
Of vibrant hues in every trail.
In unity, they share their spark,
A timeless dance from dawn till dark.

Subtle Tracings of Forgotten Lore

In the quiet of the night,
Whispers call from ancient height.
Subtle hints, a fading trace,
Stories linger, time's embrace.

Where shadows weave through silent trees,
And secrets ride upon the breeze.
Each brook and stone, a tale to tell,
In nature's arms, we know so well.

Tread softly on the forest floor,
For echoes of the past implore.
Each leaf a page, each root a thread,
A tapestry of words unsaid.

The moonlight drapes the world in dreams,
Unraveling history, it seems.
As starlit skies begin to glow,
Forgotten lore begins to flow.

In tranquil moments, listen close,
The pulse of ages, a living dose.
For every step unveils a clue,
In this realm where old meets new.

Twinkling Stories in the River's Heart

A river flows with tales untold,
Reflecting dreams like liquid gold.
Each ripple carries whispers sweet,
Life's stories dance, a rhythmic beat.

Beneath the surface, secrets hide,
Where currents shift and spirits glide.
Stars twinkle in the evening's glow,
In every wave, the world we know.

The stones below, they laugh and sigh,
With every splash, they rise and fly.
Echoes of joy in waters clear,
The river sings of love held dear.

Murmurings from the banks draw near,
As memories drift, a course sincere.
Each gentle flow and ebbing part,
Holds twinkling stories, deep in heart.

So pause and listen, heed the call,
In the river's flow, we find it all.
A woven tapestry of fate,
Where every drop illuminates.

Veiled Truths Amidst the Storm's Fury

Beneath the clouds, the tempest brews,
A symphony of wind and views.
Lightning strikes and thunder roars,
Nature's canvas paints for hours.

In the eye, a stillness gleams,
Whispers wrapped in shattered dreams.
The storm unveils its raw allure,
In chaos, we find truths obscure.

Rain falls heavy, like burdens shed,
Old fears rise, new paths to tread.
Yet through the howl, a voice persists,
A hidden strength that can't be missed.

Each gust a brush, each drop a stroke,
We learn to heal, to bend, not choke.
In swirling mists, revelations rise,
Amidst the fury, wisdom lies.

So stand your ground, embrace the fight,
In darkest hours, seek your light.
For veiled truths arise to show,
That storms may pass, but strength will grow.

Fluid Dreams on the Edges of Reality

Whispers of the night unfold,
As stars in silence dare to sing.
Dreams dance lightly, tales retold,
On edges soft, where shadows cling.

Mirrors of thought in liquid light,
Glimmering like a distant shore.
In twilight's arms, the world feels right,
As fantasies begin to soar.

Colors bleed where visions blend,
Imagined realms in swirling hue.
In every twist, a tale can bend,
To worlds where only hearts break through.

Through fragile glass, we gaze and glimpse,
The beauty caught in fleeting grace.
In each reflection, hope eclipses,
A sacred dance in time and space.

With every heartbeat, dreams ignite,
Fluid patterns, ever new.
In night's embrace, we take our flight,
In edges soft, where dreams come true.

Fleeting Moments in a Tidal Embrace

Waves crash softly on the shore,
Tides that whisper, pull away.
In fleeting dances, hearts explore,
The liquid whispers of the bay.

Each moment, like a grain of sand,
Slips through fingers, never stays.
Yet in the joy, we understand,
Life is love in countless ways.

Shells that gleam in morning's light,
Tell stories of the sea and sky.
In freedom's pulse, we see the sight,
Of dreams that echo, rise and fly.

Together, caught in nature's gown,
We breathe the air, we feel the tide.
In every crest, never a frown,
For with each wave, our souls abide.

In tides' embrace, the moments sway,
Fleeting treasures, we hold tight.
In every rise, we find our way,
Toward horizons full of light.

Chromatic Layers of Forgotten Waters

Beneath the depth, colors reside,
A canvas bled by nature's hand.
Each layer tells a tale implied,
Of time's embrace and shifting sand.

Glimmers of life in shadows play,
Hidden hues in soft refrain.
Textures swirl in a bright ballet,
Forgotten stories, yet remain.

Reflections dance on surfaces curved,
In silent whispers, memories hide.
The heart of water, ever preserved,
In chromatic grace, truths collide.

As currents weave through lonely dreams,
We dive into the depths of thought.
In vibrant shades, illusion seems,
A world where hope and love are sought.

From oh so deep, we rise and find,
The beauty in the layers' depth.
In every echo, hearts entwined,
In water's song, our thoughts are kept.

Shadows of Giants Beneath the Surface

Beneath the waves, shadows remain,
Giants of old, lost tales entwined.
In silence echo, wisdom's stain,
A presence felt, yet undefined.

With every ripple, legends breathe,
The weight of time in whispered lore.
In currents deep, we start to weave,
The stories that the waters bore.

From depths of dark, their spirits rise,
Guiding dreams that flicker and flow.
In twilight pools, the heart complies,
To dance with giants, strong and slow.

Veils of twilight, softly drawn,
Hide shadows high and shadows low.
In every dusk, a new dawn spawned,
Where ancient truths begin to show.

Together with the tides we roam,
In waters deep, where giants dwell.
In shadows cast, we find our home,
A wondrous world, a mystic spell.

Glimpses of Paradise Beneath the Roil

In shadows deep where whispers dwell,
A secret world begins to swell.
Through tempests loud, a soft embrace,
Glimmers of peace in every place.

With every wave that crashes high,
A fleeting glance of azure sky.
Amidst the chaos, colors blend,
A fragile truth that shall not end.

The roiling sea, both fierce and free,
Holds treasures masked from you and me.
In swirling tides, we seek to find,
The endless beauty, undefined.

As sunbeams dance on waters wide,
A promise formed where hopes abide.
Each rippling crest, a fleeting kiss,
A taste of pure, untainted bliss.

Within the storm, a silent call,
To dive below, to rise, to fall.
Glimpses of paradise reveal,
The love contained in every reel.

Soulful Currents in the Dragon's Breath

Beneath the roars of ancient might,
A current flows, both dark and bright.
Through fiery tides where shadows play,
The soul ignites, then drifts away.

In whispered tales of courage found,
The pulse of life, a sacred sound.
As dragons soar, their wings aglow,
They bear the weight of all we know.

With every breath, a flame ignites,
Illuminating hidden sights.
A dance of stars in swirling night,
The heart beats on, a beacon bright.

Each wave remember, tales of yore,
Of lovers lost, and paths they bore.
In dragon's breath, the spirit thrives,
Through soulful currents, love survives.

As we embrace the winds that blow,
Our stories meld, both high and low.
In this vast dance, forever blessed,
We'll seek the truth, and find our rest.

Tides of Illusion Beneath the Spray

The ocean swirls with fleeting dreams,
Where reality is not what it seems.
Beneath the spray, illusions glide,
A dance of truth we try to hide.

In every wave, a silent scream,
Reflecting back our deepest dream.
The tides will shift, the shadows play,
In liquid mirrors, lost in sway.

Bubbles rise like thoughts unspoken,
Whispers linger, bonds unbroken.
In the foam, we find our fate,
As currents twist and hearts elate.

The tide rolls in, it calls our names,
It washes over, it plays its games.
In fleeting spray, we catch a glance,
Of magic wrapped in nature's dance.

So let us float on this vast sea,
And embrace the art of being free.
Together, we'll ride the waves of change,
In tides of illusion, lives rearranged.

Illumination in the Depths of Turbulence

When storms arise, the skies turn grey,
And hope seems lost, swept far away.
In depths where shadows dwell and creep,
Illumination finds us in sleep.

Through howling winds and crashing waves,
The heart recalls what courage saves.
For even in the darkest night,
A single spark can reignite.

With every crash, a lesson learned,
In turbulence, the soul is turned.
We learn to dance, we learn to fight,
And seek the truth that brings us light.

Within the chaos, calm resides,
A beacon flashes, hope abides.
Through winding paths of strife and pain,
The glow of wisdom will remain.

So as we navigate the storm,
Embrace the tides, let love transform.
In depths of turbulence, we're bold,
For illumination turns to gold.

Serpentines of Light and Dark

In shadows where whispers play,
The serpent winds and weaves away.
Its scales reflect both day and night,
A dance of shadows, light in flight.

Through tangled paths of twisted thought,
Each turn reveals what we have sought.
In the balance of the good and vile,
The serpent smiles, beguiles with style.

With every hiss, a secret shared,
In mystic paths, we're unprepared.
The dark invites, the light enthralls,
In every twist, the mystery calls.

A journey lost in endless maze,
Where heart and mind begin to graze.
In search of truth, along its back,
The serpent coils through light and black.

Embrace the dance, the ebb and flow,
For in each shift, our spirits grow.
In serpentines of dusk and dawn,
We find our way, forever drawn.

Waves of Time Beneath a Shattered Sky

In tides that rush beyond the shore,
Time bends and twirls, forevermore.
Beneath a sky with fragments torn,
Each wave whispers of the reborn.

Colors clash, a vibrant strife,
In every crest, a piece of life.
From depths unknown, the secrets rise,
Reflecting dreams in broken skies.

The tumult roars in echoes deep,
As time unfurls, and shadows creep.
With every wave, a story told,
Beneath the sky, both young and old.

In moments lost, yet always near,
The waves of time, they hold us dear.
Each crash a pulse, a fleeting sound,
In shattered skies, we're always found.

As oceans swell and sunsets weave,
In their embrace, we dare believe.
Through every wave, we sail anew,
Beneath the shattered sky, we grew.

Riddles of the Deep in Silver Light

In depths where silence breathes a sigh,
The riddles whisper from on high.
In silver light, the shadows glide,
Secrets hide where dreams abide.

Each bubble floats, a thought in tow,
As currents twist and gently flow.
The ocean's heart beats soft and low,
In silver beams that softly glow.

What lies beneath, the deep would claim,
A world alive yet hard to name.
As silver light does guide the way,
In riddles spun, we long to stay.

With every wave, a question stirs,
In mysteries, the soul concurs.
The deep reveals what few have known,
In silver light, we walk alone.

In echoes soft, the ocean speaks,
Of journeys vast and mountain peaks.
In riddles wrapped, our spirits soar,
In silver light, forevermore.

Arteries of Motion Under a Thundering Roar

Where rivers flow with fierce delight,
The arteries pulse, both day and night.
Underneath a thundering roar,
The heartbeats echo, evermore.

With every surge, the currents leap,
In water's grasp, the secrets keep.
Through rocks and bends, they swiftly glide,
An unseen force, a restless tide.

In the dance of waves, chaos meets peace,
In motion's grip, the storms don't cease.
Each ripple sings, a storm's embrace,
As time flows on in this wild race.

Through canyons deep and valleys wide,
The arteries of life collide.
With thunder's roar, they carve the land,
In nature's hands, a steady hand.

The rhythm calls, a primal beat,
In every pulse, we find our feet.
The motion's truth forever reigns,
Underneath the roar, life gains.

Flickers of Solitude in the Spray

Amidst the mist, where shadows play,
A whisper calls, then drifts away.
The echoes linger in the breeze,
While hearts find peace beneath the trees.

A silvered drop of ocean's tear,
Balancing silence, drawing near.
A world unseen in gentle form,
In solitude's embrace, we're warm.

With every wave, the moments blend,
As time stands still, we comprehend.
The dance of water, fleeting light,
In solitude, we take our flight.

Reflections shimmer, softly shy,
In quiet depths where feelings lie.
The spray of life, a fragile art,
Awakening dreams within the heart.

Flickers of hope in the ocean's lore,
A tender pulse, forevermore.
In solitude's realm, we find our way,
Embracing the dawn of each new day.

Timeless Patterns in the Surge

Waves unfold in endless grace,
Carving stories, time can't erase.
Patterns dance upon the sea,
In every swell, a memory.

The rhythm calls, a soft refrain,
As tides weave joy, and sometimes pain.
Each surge brings forth the past anew,
In timeless flows, we're carried through.

With every crash, the echoes breath,
From depths unknown, comes life and death.
A cycle forged in nature's hand,
In whispers soft, we understand.

Harmonies of water churn and swell,
In every rise, a story to tell.
The canvas vast, in azure hue,
A dance where old and new imbue.

In twinkling light, the truth displays,
The timeless patterns of the waves.
So let us flow with every tide,
In surge's arms, let dreams abide.

Mirrored Realms in the Rainbow's Arc

Colors blend in soft embrace,
A fleeting glimpse of magic's grace.
In mirrored realms where dreams alight,
The heart ignites in pure delight.

Beneath the arc, the world's a stage,
Each hue a word, each shade a page.
The spectrum calls, inviting play,
In every glance, we find our way.

With every drop, a story paints,
In vibrant strokes, the heart then faints.
Reflections spark, revealing light,
In mirrored realms, we're close to flight.

The dance of rain and sun above,
A hymn of nature, purest love.
In colors bright, our hopes arise,
As magic flows beneath the skies.

In every curve, a secret hides,
In mirrored worlds, the spirit glides.
So chase the hues, let laughter soar,
In rainbow's arc, forevermore.

Harmonies of Chaos Beneath the Waves

In depths unknown, the whispers sound,
A symphony in chaos found.
With every rise, a thrill ignites,
In darkened depths, the spirit fights.

The tides collide, a wild dance,
Nature's pulse invites a chance.
In swirling currents, life unfurls,
As harmony within chaos swirls.

Beneath the surface, tempests roar,
In every crash, we seek for more.
The ocean's breath, both calm and fierce,
In tangled threads, our souls it pierce.

From shadowed depths, we rise and glide,
With every wave, a hidden guide.
For in the chaos, beauty sings,
The harmony of life it brings.

In dance of foam, we find our place,
Amidst the storm, we learn to face.
In depths of chaos, trust the way,
For there, the soul begins to play.

Caverns of Light in the Grumbling Depths

In shadows deep, the whispers play,
Where echoes forge the night from day.
A dance of light, a flickering flame,
Illuminates the caverns' name.

Beneath the stone, where silence sleeps,
The heart of mystery softly weeps.
Crystals beam like stars at night,
Within the dark, they spark with light.

A winding path through earth and time,
The grumbling depths, a secret chime.
With every step, the world expands,
As visions bloom in shadowed lands.

Amidst the gloom, a beacon shines,
Guiding dreams through twisted mines.
In caverns vast, where echoes blend,
The journey's start, it knows no end.

So step with care in this mystique,
Where deep-rooted thoughts begin to speak.
The light within the dark does dwell,
In caverns of light, we weave our spell.

Ephemeral Pathways Through the Mist

In morning's breath, the fog weaves tight,
A tapestry of whispers, faint light.
Footfalls echo on the dampened ground,
Where secrets linger, yet to be found.

Each step unfolds a story untold,
Pathways shifting, as the day grows old.
Through veils of grey, a silhouette roams,
Chasing shadows, seeking lost homes.

In the mist, clarity hides away,
Yet beckons onward, urging to stay.
A fleeting moment, lost in the haze,
Capturing time in a delicate daze.

Transitory beauty, a soft retreat,
As daylight breaks, and illusions greet.
Through ephemeral paths, we learn to trust,
The way of the world, in shadows and dust.

So walk with wonder, let your heart lead,
For in every mist, new destinies breed.
The whispers of life, through time's gentle twist,
Guide us on pathways through the mist.

Unveiled Dreams in the Churning Flow

In rivers deep, where waters swirl,
Lies the promise of a hidden world.
Dreams awaken in the churning tide,
Revealing truths we often hide.

The current pulls, a gentle sway,
Carrying wishes, lost and stray.
With every ripple, hopes arise,
Unveiling visions, bright like skies.

A tapestry of desires unspools,
Among the depths, fate gently fuels.
In the flow, we find our way,
Ebbing and flowing, night and day.

Through turbulent waves, we learn to see,
The essence of our yearning hearts free.
And as we drift, we come to know,
Our unveiled dreams in the churning flow.

So let the waters guide your mind,
Through all the shadows left behind.
For in the river's ceaseless glow,
Lie the dreams we've yet to show.

Glimmers of Eternity on Water's Edge

At water's brink, the cosmos stirs,
With glimmers bright, the silence purrs.
Reflections dance in the evening light,
A moment captured, pure delight.

Each ripple holds a story spun,
Of ancient nights and glowing sun.
A fleeting glance, yet vast and wide,
In depths where timeless secrets bide.

The horizon glows, a painted dream,
Unfolding tales as soft waves gleam.
Eternity whispers on the breeze,
In nature's arms, the heart finds ease.

Among the reeds, the silence bends,
Where every echo softly lends.
To fleeting moments, we hold tight,
Glimmers of eternity in the night.

So linger here, where dreams converge,
As every heartbeat starts to surge.
At water's edge, we learn to see,
The glimmers of what's meant to be.

The Beauty of Chaos in Stillness

In quiet corners, shadows merge,
Whispers of wind, a subtle urge.
Colors dance without a sound,
In the stillness, chaos found.

Gentle rhythms of the night,
Stars above, a scattered light.
The heart beats in muted grace,
In silence, we find our place.

A single leaf falls to the ground,
Nature's secrets softly bound.
Within the calm, wild dreams ignite,
The beauty of chaos, pure delight.

Echoes linger, thoughts intertwine,
In the pause, we draw a line.
Living in this fleeting breath,
Chaos dances close to death.

Yet in stillness, we embrace,
Life's complexities we trace.
And in the quiet, we release,
The beauty thrives, the heart finds peace.

Echos of Yesterday in Rippling Waters

Ripples dance upon the lake,
Carrying tales that time can't shake.
Whispers float on gentle waves,
Echos of souls, the water saves.

In twilight's glow, memories gleam,
Images fade, like a fleeting dream.
Fish dart fast beneath the sky,
In liquid lanes, the past runs dry.

Against the shore, the moments crash,
Fragments of light in a brilliant flash.
Each drop tells stories, lost yet found,
In rippling waters, we are bound.

The moon reflects, a silver guide,
Through currents deep, where secrets hide.
Yesterday's sighs now blend and blur,
In every wave, our hearts confer.

Listen close, let the waters speak,
In their embrace, the wise grow meek.
Time flows on, yet we remain,
In rippling waters, joy and pain.

Breath of the Earth in the Serenade

Upon the breeze, a soft refrain,
Nature's hymn, a sweet sustain.
From mountain high to valley low,
The breath of earth, a gentle flow.

Whispers rise in morning light,
Dew-kissed leaves, a pure delight.
Birds take flight on wings of song,
In their chorus, we belong.

The rustling trees, they sway and bend,
A melody that has no end.
Crickets join as shadows creep,
In twilight's arms, the world falls asleep.

Rivers hum a soothing tune,
Underneath the watchful moon.
Each heartbeat matches nature's grace,
In harmony, we find our place.

With every breath, life shares its song,
In endless rhythms, we belong.
The serenade, a timeless art,
Breath of the earth within the heart.

Veil of Dreams in the Churning Tide

In the ocean's depths, shadows play,
Secrets wrapped in foamy spray.
The tide pulls forth, then back again,
A veil of dreams, where hopes remain.

Currents weave through silent fears,
Carrying wishes, lost in tears.
With every wave, a story told,
In the churning tide, both brave and bold.

Moonlit nights spark reflections bright,
Illusions shimmer in soft twilight.
Beneath the surface, hearts collide,
In the dance of the churning tide.

Breaths held tight in salty air,
Echoes whisper, a timeless prayer.
The ocean sings, its tantalizing call,
Within its depths, we rise, we fall.

Yet in the chaos, dreams take flight,
Guided by stars, through dark to light.
The veil of dreams, both fierce and wide,
In the embrace of the churning tide.

Elysian Whispers Among the Reeds

Softly the winds begin to sigh,
Among the reeds where secrets lie.
Each rustle tells a tale of old,
In whispered tones, a truth unfolds.

Beneath the sky, a canvas wide,
Nature's voice, a calm guide.
The sunlight dances, shadows play,
In harmony, they drift away.

Ripples cradle fleeting thoughts,
As life and time entwine in knots.
A soft embrace, the heart can feel,
In moments cherished, ever real.

The reeds lean close, a gentle sway,
Holding dreams that drift astray.
Elysian calls in twilight's glow,
Awake the spirits, let them know.

In silence, find the beauty there,
In every breath, a whispered prayer.
The world unfolds, a tender grace,
Elysian whispers, time's embrace.

Chromatic Echoes in Undercurrents

In shadows where the colors blend,
Echoes stir, the sights transcend.
Chromatic waves of sound and light,
Undercurrents dance, igniting night.

A canvas splashed with hues so bright,
Painted dreams take wondrous flight.
With every pulse, the rhythm flows,
In vibrant whispers, the heart knows.

Beneath the surface, stories hide,
In chromatic depths, where secrets bide.
A tune awakens, takes its hold,
Every note a tale retold.

The colors swirl, a tempest's spin,
Each echo rings within the skin.
In fleeting moments yet to pass,
Time bends softly, like fine glass.

So let the waves of sound resound,
In chromatic echoes, joy is found.
A symphony of life and art,
Where every color speaks to the heart.

Mirage of Memories in a Thundering Rush

In the landscape of a fleeting dream,
Mirages form, like soft moonbeam.
Whispers haunt the corners of thought,
In a rush of time, they're gently caught.

Memories dance on a thunderous sound,
Echoes ripple, lost yet found.
The tempest brews in a wistful haze,
A heart recalls the golden days.

Through fleeting shadows, figures race,
Fingers trace a bygone space.
In every heartbeat, stories bloom,
A poignant pulse, beyond the gloom.

In the rush of life, we chase the past,
Seeing glimmers, too vibrant to last.
A mirage lingers, a gentle touch,
Whispers of what meant so much.

Yet time is swift, a river flows,
Through thundering rush, each moment goes.
With every echo, the heart will cling,
To mirages, memories that still sing.

Illuminated Pathways in Gloom

In twilight's grasp, where shadows rest,
Illuminated pathways put to test.
A tender light begins to spread,
Guiding footsteps where dreams are led.

Through darkened woods, the stars ignite,
A soft embrace, a beacon bright.
With every step, the heart finds peace,
In luminescence, fears release.

The night unfolds with whispered grace,
In pathways bright, we find our place.
A dance of glow among the trees,
Illuminated thoughts, like gentle breeze.

As shadows weave their tales of old,
A journey beckons, brave and bold.
With every spark, new worlds arise,
Illuminated visions in twilight skies.

So walk the paths where light invites,
In glowing moments, life ignites.
Through gloom and doubt, the heartache fades,
Illuminated pathways, where hope pervades.

Ripples of Fire on a Liquid Mirror

A dance of flames on mirrored glass,
Whispers of warmth in night's embrace.
Stars reflect in liquid blaze,
The world transformed, a glowing space.

Embers leap with a joyful cry,
Flickering light in the evening's sigh.
Each ripple tells a secret tale,
Of dreams ignited, hearts set sail.

The moon looks down with silvery gaze,
Guiding shadows in a fiery maze.
As flickers fade into the dark,
Hope rekindles with every spark.

The water holds a thousand flames,
Ebbing tides call out their names.
In the silence, we hear them sing,
A symphony of passion's fling.

The fire dances, a fleeting show,
In liquid mirror, the wild winds blow.
An echo of warmth that will remain,
A memory of joy, a sweet refrain.

Luminous Cracks in the Emerald Depths

In oceans deep where shadows dwell,
Luminous cracks weave tales to tell.
Emerald whispers call with grace,
Secrets shelter in this hidden place.

Fins flicker through the light's embrace,
Graceful movements in tranquil space.
Each beam reveals a world unknown,
Where depths of dreams have always grown.

Glimmers dance on ancient stones,
A treasure trove of hushed undertones.
Echoes of life in vibrant hues,
Crimson threads in twilight's blues.

Emerging from the glassy tide,
An enigma where wonders bide.
The sea's heart beats with a glow,
In the whispers of currents slow.

The twilight weaves its emerald cloak,
In every ripple, a story spoke.
In the depths, we find our fears,
Yet luminous cracks call forth our tears.

Scale-Laden Secrets Beneath the Tide

Beneath the waves, a world concealed,
Scale-laden secrets, softly revealed.
Aquatic dreams in shadows blend,
Whispers of wonders that never end.

Each creature glides with fluid grace,
Weaving stories in their space.
Echoes of life through currents flow,
In the deep, mysteries gracefully grow.

Teeth of coral and shells that gleam,
Hold the tales of the ocean's dream.
A language spoken in hues bright,
Where day meets dusk in dream's delight.

Anemones sway with a gentle touch,
Each motion speaks of depths so much.
The ocean's heart beats strong and true,
A cradle for dreams, both old and new.

In the silence, a symphony plays,
Of scale and fin in watery ways.
A treasure trove of hidden tales,
In the dance of tides, the mystery prevails.

A Symphony of Liquid Splendor

In flowing streams, the water flows,
A symphony where nature shows.
Each ripple sings a soft refrain,
A melody of joy and pain.

The sunlight sparkles, golden bright,
Creating diamonds in the light.
Songbirds join in sweet accord,
Nature's heartbeats, never ignored.

Leaves whisper secrets to the breeze,
A harmony that aims to please.
In every drop, a world exists,
Where dreams take flight, where hope persists.

The wind carries notes both near and far,
Guiding us gently like a star.
In currents deep, emotions swell,
A story woven, weaves its spell.

Each wave composes its own part,
A testament of life and art.
Together, they create the song,
A symphony where we belong.

Shattered Reflections in Mist

Ghostly shapes in morning light,
Whispers trapped in soft twilight.
Mirrors break, yet still remain,
Fragments scattered, like the rain.

Echoes ripple through the haze,
Time unwinds in gentle ways.
Every shard holds a lost tale,
Secrets buried, dreams set sail.

Flickering visions start to blend,
A canvas kissed by nature's hand.
Patterns dance on waters deep,
Memories wake from restless sleep.

Softened edges melt away,
Hope and sorrow in the fray.
As the mist begins to clear,
Shattered pieces draw us near.

Through the fog, we seek to find,
Pieces of our hearts combined.
In the stillness, echoes play,
Shattered dreams, yet here we stay.

Echoes of Scales and Water

Beneath the waves, a world conceals,
Echoes dance, in twisting reels.
Scales that shimmer, colors bright,
Flashes glinting in the light.

Whispers of the ocean's breath,
Life and mystery, dance with death.
Ripples trace the joy and pain,
Every drop, a soft refrain.

Fins that glide through cool embrace,
Nature's rhythm finds its place.
A symphony of silent calls,
Underneath where darkness falls.

Waves that clash and softly sigh,
Echoes rise and gently die.
Scales, like secrets, gleam and wane,
In this sea, both loss and gain.

In the depths, we contemplate,
Harmony that we create.
Through water's lens, we see our part,
Echoes of the ocean's heart.

Veins of Light beneath the Surf

Underneath the ocean's crest,
Veins of light find their own rest.
Slips of gold and sapphire hues,
Painting tales in silent views.

Currents pulse with every wave,
A glimmering path that we crave.
Mysteries in shadows play,
In the depths, the light will stay.

Flickering rays like whispered dreams,
Dancing softly in the beams.
Moments captured, time unfurls,
Secrets held in watery swirls.

Tides that ebb and flow with grace,
Shining threads in ocean's embrace.
Veins of light sing to the deep,
Awakening the souls that sleep.

With each rise, the beauty flows,
Nature's art, where magic grows.
Beneath the surf, we find our way,
Veins of light, where shadows play.

Whispers of Wings over Shimmering Waves

Whispers travel on the breeze,
Wings that flutter, hearts that freeze.
Over waves that shine and sway,
Nature's song, the night and day.

Feathers brush the ocean's face,
A gentle touch, a soft embrace.
Reflections glisten, tales unfold,
Every moment, stories told.

Sails that catch the vibrant hue,
Birds in flight, a world anew.
Their calls echo through the air,
A symphony beyond compare.

With each landing, stillness reigns,
Peaceful hearts cast off their chains.
Waves that shimmer, wings that glide,
In this dance, we turn the tide.

As the sunset paints the sky,
Whispers mingle, soft and shy.
Over shimmering waves we soar,
In this moment, hearts explore.

Cascading Whispers in the Moonlight

Underneath the silver glow,
Soft whispers rise and flow.
Gentle breezes start to dance,
Nature's sweet, enchanted trance.

The nightingale begins to sing,
While shadows swirl and cling.
Stars twinkle in delight,
Guiding dreams into the night.

Rippling waters softly gleam,
Mirroring a mystic dream.
The world feels calm and still,
As moonlight bends to every will.

In this space of soft embrace,
Time drifts by without a trace.
Heartbeats echo in the dark,
Crafting magic, leaving marks.

Cascading whispers, secrets shared,
Moments cherished, deeply cared.
Moonlit paths, so bright and clear,
Cradle dreams and hold them near.

Serenade of Echoes in the Echoing Divide

Voices rise within the void,
Melodies softly deployed.
Each note meets the endless air,
A rhythmic dance beyond compare.

In the mountains, echoes play,
Carrying memories away.
Whispers linger on the breeze,
Finding rest within the trees.

Harmonics weave a timeless tale,
In valleys deep and hills so pale.
Nature's hand, a steady guide,
Leading hearts through the divide.

Waves of sound, a gentle tide,
In silence, spirits coincide.
As shadows stretch and bend,
The serenade shall never end.

In this realm where echoes bloom,
Music fills the spacious room.
Together, we shall find our voice,
In the echoes, we rejoice.

Essence of the Abyss in a Gentle Spray

Down below, the waters churn,
In the depths, the lanterns burn.
Whispers rise from shadowed caves,
Guided by the ebbing waves.

Soft currents pulse and reveal,
Secrets that the depths conceal.
Each drop tells of ancient lore,
Stories kept forevermore.

Gentle spray, like mist at dawn,
Awakens dreams that linger on.
In the abyss, life finds its way,
Color blooms in shades of gray.

Through the darkness, whispers glide,
Carrying the heart's true pride.
Every wave, a chance to breathe,
In the depths, we find belief.

Essence flows, a world anew,
In the dark, a shining cue.
Gentle spray, a tender kiss,
In the abyss lies tranquil bliss.

Muted Colors in the Great Journey

In twilight hues, the day departs,
Softening the weary hearts.
Muted colors blend and sway,
Guiding us along the way.

With every step, we roam and seek,
Wisdom whispered, truth unique.
Paths unfold beneath our feet,
In every corner, life's heartbeat.

Gentle shadows cast their spell,
Telling tales we dare not tell.
In silence, we find our grace,
Lost within the soft embrace.

The journey winds through hills and streams,
Weaving together hopes and dreams.
Muted colors, vast and wide,
Hold our fears and joys inside.

Through every rise and every fall,
We gather strength, we heed the call.
In muted shades, we find the light,
Embracing darkness, seeking bright.

Serpent Dance in Crystal Foam

In the moon's soft glow, they sway,
A serpentine rhythm in the bay.
Whispers weave through waves that gleam,
As water dances in a dream.

Tails glisten bright with silver hue,
They twist and turn, a vibrant view.
Beneath the stars, they spin and glide,
In crystal foam, they slip and slide.

Ancient tales in currents flow,
Of dancers lost, now free to show.
The ocean's pulse, in sync they find,
A harmony of wave and wind.

Each flicker bright, a flash of grace,
In liquid light, they find their place.
A fleeting moment, forever held,
In crystal foam, their stories meld.

As dawn approaches, they fade away,
The serpent dance, the night holds sway.
Yet in the heart, their movements remain,
A memory wrapped in ocean's vein.

Fractured Dreams on a Silver Sea

Beneath the shadows, whispers sigh,
Fractured dreams in twilight lie.
Rippling waves, reflections torn,
Lost in silence, hope reborn.

The silver sea, a canvas wide,
Holds secrets deep, where fears abide.
Ghostly ships in misty night,
Glide through visions, taking flight.

Each splintered thought, a starless plight,
Sails of despair against the light.
Yet in the depths, a glow persists,
A beacon bright, through the fog, it twists.

With every tide, the dreams reshift,
Pieces scattered, a burdensome gift.
But hope remains, a steadfast key,
Unlocking hearts upon the sea.

As dawn draws near, the darkness wanes,
Fractured dreams hold gentle chains.
A silver sea whispers anew,
Of brighter shores, where skies are blue.

Kaleidoscope of Dragonfly Shadows

In twilight's glow, where colors blend,
Dragonflies dance, their wings extend.
A kaleidoscope, vibrant and bright,
Whirling patterns, a joyous flight.

Shadows flicker on the ground,
In every movement, dreams are found.
Gossamer wings brush the air,
Echoes of laughter, light as prayer.

Among the reeds, they flit and play,
A delicate game at close of day.
Each shimmer tells a story told,
Of days forgotten, of memories bold.

As night descends, their colors fade,
But in the heart, their hues invade.
In whispers soft, their spirits roam,
A kaleidoscope that brings us home.

The magic lingers in the dusk,
Transforming shadows, without husk.
A dance of life, where time stands still,
In dragonfly dreams, we find our will.

The Chill of Celestial Breath

In the stillness of the night,
Comes a chill, a soft delight.
Breath of stars in hushed retreat,
Whispers cold, yet bittersweet.

Veils of mist weave through the trees,
A cosmic breeze, a gentle tease.
Each shimmer holds a distant tale,
Of galaxies where wonders sail.

In silver light, the world transforms,
As celestial breath in silence warms.
A moment held, where time suspends,
In frozen air, the spirit bends.

The darkness deep, yet full of grace,
Embraces all in its embrace.
A dance of shadows, soft and bright,
In the chill of this endless night.

Awake to realms beyond the skies,
Where dreams take flight, and never die.
In the chill, we find our worth,
A cosmic sigh, the pulse of Earth.

Where Dragons Print Their Secrets in Sand

In twilight's breath, they dance and glide,
Upon the dunes, where shadows abide.
Footprints traced, a legend's sign,
In hidden depths, their tales entwine.

With whispering winds that softly sigh,
Ancient secrets that never die.
In grains of gold, their stories lie,
Beneath the watchful, starlit sky.

Eternal flames ignite the night,
With scales aglow, a wondrous sight.
Through sandstorms fierce, they seek their kin,
Where shadows dance and dreams begin.

A tapestry of fire and lore,
In every grain, a tale to explore.
The sands bear witness, soft yet grand,
To the dragons' print upon the land.

From dusk till dawn, their spirits roam,
In rugged winds, they find their home.
In whispers low, legends expand,
Where dragons print their secrets in sand.

Mesmerizing Glints of Forgotten Lore

In twilight realms where shadows play,
The glints of gold beckon and sway.
Ancient whispers weave through the air,
Tales of glory and heart's despair.

Worn tomes lay beneath dust's embrace,
Each page a journey, a sacred place.
Fragments of dreams, lost in the night,
Bring forth the past with shimmering light.

The moonlight casts its silver sheen,
On rivers of time, where few have been.
Memories flicker like stars in the dark,
In hearts of seekers, they leave a mark.

With every step on this ancient ground,
Echoes of wisdom resonate sound.
Each sigh of wind, a song once sung,
Melodies of old forever young.

In these glints, the lost are found,
Dreams reclaim their sacred ground.
The past ignites with vibrant power,
In mesmerizing glints of forgotten lore.

Tempestuous Dragons and Sparkling Veins

In the roar of storms, they take to the air,
Tempestuous dragons, bold and rare.
With lightning in their grasp, they soar,
Through thunder's song, forevermore.

In caves where jewels gleam and shine,
Sparkling veins of magic intertwine.
Deep within the earth's embrace,
Dragons guard this sacred space.

Flames dance high with fierce desire,
Through tempest winds, they never tire.
Each heartbeat echoes, strong and wild,
In the heart of nature, they are riled.

With scales that shimmer, fierce and bright,
They bring forth dawn from endless night.
In every roar, a tale expressed,
The tempest's touch, a heart impressed.

Where fire and storm in harmony meet,
A symphony of power, strong and sweet.
In every gust, in every strain,
Tempestuous dragons and sparkling veins.

Celestial Tides in Shattered Harmony

Beneath the moon's soft, tender glow,
Celestial tides begin to flow.
In rhythmic waves that ebb and crest,
A dance of stars, a cosmic quest.

But shattered harmony breaks the night,
As shadows flicker and take flight.
In silence deep, the heart does ache,
For dreams that fade, for bonds that break.

The ocean's whisper tells a tale,
Of ships long lost and hearts so frail.
In every grain of sand, a sigh,
Of hopes that soared, yet choose to die.

Yet still, the tides heave and weave,
In every swell, new dreams conceive.
Above the chaos, stars draw near,
Guiding whispers through darkened fear.

In celestial dance, a path appears,
To find the strength beyond our tears.
Through shattered chords, harmonies rise,
Celestial tides in shattered skies.

Shattered Reflections in Mist

In twilight's cool embrace we stand,
Shadows flicker, softly kissed by night.
Mirrors fractured in the dampened land,
Echoes whisper secrets of lost light.

Figures dance in veils of swirling grey,
Glimmers fade, then surge like restless tides.
What was once clear now drifts away,
Clarity lost where solitude abides.

Fleeting moments ripple like the stream,
An image caught, then whisked from our sight.
Doubt drapes over even the strongest dream,
In shattered glass, truth escapes the night.

A ghostly path where footprints dissolve,
We chase the phantoms of what has been.
In misty realms, our hearts try to resolve,
The depths of sorrow hidden within.

But every shard holds a tale in its gleam,
Each fragment pulses with a gentle breath.
Though lost in fog, there lies a shared theme,
Beauty persists, even in the death.

Shimmering Craters Beneath the Storm

Lightning dances in a jarring sky,
While thunder roars like a beast untamed.
Craters glisten, catching every sigh,
Nature's fury, both wild and unnamed.

Rain falls like stories from realms afar,
Each drop a whisper, a tale unspun.
A tapestry woven with dreams of stars,
And in the tempest, new life begun.

In the chaos, a beauty resides,
Reflections shimmer where shadows creep.
The earth, a canvas where hope abides,
Beneath the striking storm, secrets keep.

Each crater tells of a world reborn,
After the tempest, in softening light.
Wounds of the sky with colors adorn,
A promise of peace in the lingering night.

So let the storm crash, let nature sing,
Through raging winds, our spirits shall soar.
In shimmering craters, the heart takes wing,
Finding joy as the heavens explore.

Mysteries Beneath the Waterfall's Veil

A silken cascade falls with grace so rare,
Veiling secrets in its flowing embrace.
As whispers softly linger in the air,
Boundless wonders dare us to trace.

Beneath the surface, stories intertwine,
Fish glide through shadows, a world untouched.
Ancient echoes in the depths define,
Life's rhythm pulses, ever clutched.

Drifting leaves swirl in the gentle mist,
Colors shimmer, blending earth and sky.
In every droplet, a tale persists,
The wisdom of ages, forever nigh.

Amidst the rush, a tranquil heart beats slow,
In moments fleeting, stillness at play.
A labyrinth hidden where few dare to go,
Unraveling truths in the light of day.

So stand before the veil, breathe it in,
Embrace the wonders that call from below.
For mysteries whisper where journeys begin,
In the flow of the waterfall's gentle flow.

Ethereal Traces of Wind's Breath

Softly the zephyrs weave through the trees,
Carrying whispers of stories untold.
In their embrace, we find tranquil ease,
Ethereal traces, a caress so bold.

Dancing with petals, they sway and twirl,
Like secrets exchanged in a lover's sigh.
Breath of the heavens, soft as a pearl,
Guiding the starlight as night draws nigh.

Over the mountains, they wisp and glide,
Stretching the fabric of twilight's grace.
In corridors whispered, they gently bide,
Painting the dusk with an airy lace.

Through fields of gold where the wildflowers sway,
Their gentle lullabies churn and entwine.
Carving a path, they dance through the day,
Eternal, unseen, yet vividly divine.

So let the wind carry your dreams alight,
Feel the invisible caress on your skin.
In every sigh born of the night,
Find the ethereal traces, let them begin.

www.ingramcontent.com/pod-product-compliance
Ingram Content Group UK Ltd.
Pitfield, Milton Keynes, MK11 3LW, UK
UKHW021536210125
4208UKWH00025B/678

9 781805 597872